TETON COUNTY LIBRARY
JACKSON, WYOMING

ATLAS OF MINIATURE ADVENTURES

WIDE EYED EDITIONS

North
America

Central
America

Afric

South
America

WORLD
MAP

CONTENTS

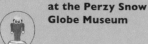

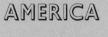
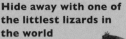

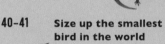

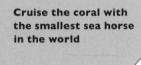

THE WORLD IS FULL OF MINI MARVELS . . .

Big things get a lot of attention: the planet's longest rivers, tallest mountains, and highest buildings are tourist hot spots, featured in record books the world over. But what about the small things?

This book celebrates life's little wonders, from the world's tiniest animals to its miniature works of art, intricate model villages, pint-sized plants, teeny toys, and even its smallest countries. These mini marvels show that the best—and the quirkiest—things really do come in small packages.

EUROPE

From model villages and mini museums to the world's smallest country, Europe is packed full of wee wonders waiting to be discovered.

Iceland

Faroe Islands

Shetland Islands

Strum along with the
UKULELE ORCHESTRA OF
GREAT BRITAIN (UK)

Ride in the Peel P50,
the SMALLEST CAR
IN THE WORLD
(Isle of Man, UK)

See Holland
in miniature at
MADURODAM
(Netherlands)

Nor

Ireland

United
Kingdom

Netherlands

Take a trip back in time at
BEKONSCOT MODEL VILLAGE (UK)

Belgium   Luxembo

Explore a continent
in miniature at
MINI-EUROPE
(Belgium)

North Atlantic Ocean

Play the
giant at the
MUSÉE
MINIATURE
(France)

France

Switzerland

Liechtenstein

It

Think outside the
box at the
MATCHBOX MUSEUM
(Portugal)

Monaco

San
Ma

Portugal

Spain

Mediterranean
Sea

Corsica

Balearic
Islands

Sardini

White Sea

Finland

Russia

weden

Baltic Sea

Estonia

Gotland

Latvia

Lithuania

Kaliningrad Oblast

Belarus

Tee off in the dark at
BLACK LIGHT MINI GOLF
(Germany)

Czech
Republic

Poland

Ukraine

Shake things up at the
PERZY SNOW
GLOBE MUSEUM
(Austria)

Slovakia

Moldova

Marvel at the
MUSEUM OF
MICRO-ART
(Hungary)

Hungary

Romania

Croatia

Serbia

Black
Sea

Asia

Bosnia &
Herzegovina

Montenegro

Kosovo

Macedonia

Bulgaria

Turkey

Albania

Greece

Turkey

Visit the SMALLEST
COUNTRY IN THE WORLD
(Vatican City)

Discover Miniatürk,
the world's LARGEST
MINIATURE PARK (Turkey)

Sicily

Malta

Cyprus

9

Bekonscot has welcomed over 14 million visitors since 1929, including the Queen, who used to visit on her birthday as a child.

BUCKINGHAMSHIRE, UK

The railway that runs through Bekonscot is one of the largest model railways in the UK.

TAKE A TRIP BACK IN TIME AT
BEKONSCOT MODEL VILLAGE

Welcome to a miniature wonderland! The world's first model village opened in 1929 in the garden of British accountant Roland Callingham. Now, 90 years later, this picture-perfect 1930s time warp has more than 200 mini buildings, 1,000 animals, thousands of tiny inhabitants, and hundreds of moving vehicles and models. There are houses, castles, farms, docks, a railway, a racecourse, a fairground, and even a burning cottage. The scenes are crammed with little details to spot, so keep your eyes peeled!

3,000 tiny people go about their daily business in Bekonscot.

In 1952, the teenage Princess Beatrix was appointed mayor of Madurodam. Now a new mayor is elected every year from a "city council" of local schoolchildren.

Madurodam's mini residents change with the seasons: in summer they wear T-shirts, and in winter they dress warm.

THE HAGUE, THE NETHERLANDS

12

Much of the Netherlands lies low sea level. Madurodam's little canals and dikes tell the story of the nation's ongoing battle to keep the waters at bay.

Legend has it that a boy plugged a hole in a leaking dike to save Madurodam from flooding.

SEE HOLLAND IN MINIATURE AT
MADURODAM

Where can you pilot a tiny plane, load containers onto a cargo ship, operate a storm surge barrier, and bid at a flower auction? All in the miniature city of Madurodam! This shrunk-down town was built in 1952 and has attracted millions of visitors ever since. Here you can find tiny versions of the Netherlands' historic buildings and landmarks, as well as tulip fields, cheese markets, canal-side houses, and windmills. A tiny world of Dutch delights awaits.

TEE OFF IN THE DARK AT
BLACK LIGHT MINI GOLF

This is mini golf as you've never seen it before. Tucked away beneath Berlin's Görlitzer Park, in the cellar of an old train station, are 18 holes of miniature glow-in-the-dark fun. In this crazily-colored neon world, you can hit your golf ball past famous Berlin landmarks, through strange undersea scenes, and into futuristic space-age landscapes. Get putting!

BERLIN, GERMANY

Take your pick from this wacky collection of balls. Eyeball, anyone?

Wear 3-D glasses to make the scenery come to life!

The scenes contain thousands of tiny details, including fake mold on the walls and peeling paintwork.

Each object is carefully positioned to look true to life.

Magnifying glasses are on hand to help visitors appreciate the mini masterpieces!

PLAY THE GIANT AT THE

MUSÉE MINIATURE

This quirky museum presents over 100 super-realistic miniature scenes. Visitors can discover a world of tiny wonders, from a scaled-down natural history museum to an elegant Parisian restaurant; from a dusty, abandoned theater to a trendy New York apartment, and even the inside of a gloomy prison. Each tiny scene takes months of hard work to research and build by hand. Prepare to be impressed.

SHAKE THINGS UP AT THE

PERZY SNOW GLOBE MUSEUM

Snow globes were invented in 1900 by an Austrian named Erwin Perzy, who made surgical instruments. He was trying to increase the brightness of a lightbulb by placing a glass globe in front of it, filled with water. He experimented by adding grains of white powder to the water to reflect the light, and the snow globe was born! Today, visitors to this Vienna museum can learn about the history of these miniature winter wonderlands in the place where it all began.

The recipe for the fake snow is a closely guarded secret!

VIENNA, AUSTRIA

18

Erwin Perzy's grandson now runs the company, which produces about 200,000 snow globes a year.

Perzy's first snow globe contained a tiny model of Austria's Mariazell Basilica.

The museum has a replica of a snow globe made for U.S. president Bill Clinton, containing real confetti from his inauguration.

AFRICA

Safari lovers will have heard of Africa's "Big Five" animals, but this vast continent is also home to some incredible tiny creatures, as well as some very ancient miniature monuments.

Madeira

Canary Islands

Morocco

Western Sahara

Mauritania

Mali

Cape Verde

Senegal

The Gambia

Guinea-Bissau

Guinea

Burkina Fa

Sierra Leone

Ivory Coast

Gh

Liberia

North Atlantic Ocean

Wallow with the
PYGMY HIPPOS
(Liberia)

Bow to the tiny
ROYAL ANTELOPE
(Ghana)

Ascension Island

Plod along with the
SMALLEST TORTOISE
IN THE WORLD
(Namibia)

St. Helena

South Atlantic Ocean

Stop off at the
OUTENIQUA MOD
RAILWAY
(South Africa)

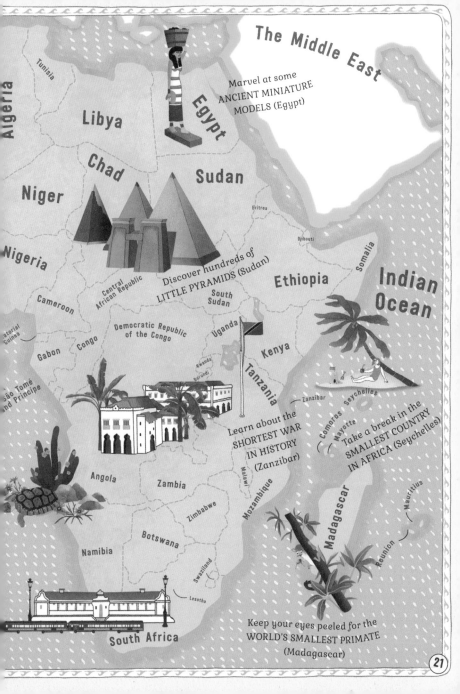

Tunisia

Algeria

Libya

Egypt

Marvel at some
ANCIENT MINIATURE
MODELS (Egypt)

Chad

Sudan

Niger

Eritrea

Nigeria

Djibouti

Cameroon

Central
African Republic

Discover hundreds of
LITTLE PYRAMIDS (Sudan)

South
Sudan

Ethiopia

Somalia

Indian
Ocean

Equatorial
Guinea

Gabon   Congo

Democratic Republic
of the Congo

Uganda

Kenya

Rwanda

Burundi

Tanzania

São Tomé
and Principe

Zanzibar

Comoros   Seychelles

Mayotte

Take a break in the
SMALLEST COUNTRY
IN AFRICA (Seychelles)

Learn about the
SHORTEST WAR
IN HISTORY
(Zanzibar)

Angola

Zambia

Malawi

Mozambique

Madagascar

Mauritius

Zimbabwe

Botswana

Namibia

Reunion

Swaziland

Lesotho

South Africa

Keep your eyes peeled for the
WORLD'S SMALLEST PRIMATE
(Madagascar)

WORLD'S SMALLEST PRIMATE

On a moonlit night in Madagascar's Kirindy Forest, you may be lucky enough to spot an extraordinary creature scampering through the trees. Compared to its ape and monkey cousins, Madame Berthe's mouse lemur is minuscule. This tiny primate is so small that it could easily fit inside a teacup. It has an average body length of 3.5 inches, and weighs about 30 grams—about the same as a slice of bread!

To mark its territory, the mouse lemur pees on its hands, then plants smelly handprints along tree branches!

A baby mouse lemur's tiny hands are perfect for grasping branches.

This tiny lemur is in danger because the forest where it lives is under threat.

KIRINDY FOREST, MADAGASCAR

Madame Berthe's mouse lemur
is hunted by snakes, owls,
and even other lemurs.

NAMIBIA & SOUTH AFRICA

This little tortoise spends most of the summer and winter hiding away, but it comes out in spring to feed on juicy plants.

PLOD ALONG WITH THE

SMALLEST TORTOISE IN THE WORLD

Living on the rocky hillsides of South Africa and Namibia is a teeny, tiny tortoise. The speckled padloper is a hardy survivor, sheltering from blistering summer sun or freezing winter temperatures in rocky crevices. Thought to be the smallest tortoise in the world, the male speckled padloper is tiny enough to hold in the palm of your hand!

A full-grown male measures only about 2.8 inches; females are slightly larger.

The padloper's mottled shell helps disguise it in the rocky landscape.

Arctic Ocean

Greenland

Davis Strait

Alaska (USA)

Go sandboarding in the SMALLEST DESERT IN THE WORLD (Canada)

Gulf of Alaska

Hudson Bay

Canada

Get burrowing with the PYGMY RABBIT (USA)

Send a letter with the WORLD'S SMALLEST POSTAL SERVICE (USA)

Visit small-town America at the ROADSIDE AMERICA MODEL VILLAGE (USA)

United States of America

Take a peek at one of the WORLD'S SMALLEST BUTTERFLIES (USA)

Mexico

Take a little bite of a tiny MEXICAN CUCUMBER (Mexico)

Gulf of Mexico

North Pacific Ocean

NORTH AMERICA

North America's little landmarks are big in personality, from one of the world's largest model railways to the planet's most lavish dollhouse—and don't forget those mini presidents!

Discover one of the WORLD'S SMALLEST DINOSAUR FOOTPRINTS (Canada)

North Atlantic Ocean

Discover one of the WORLD'S LARGEST MODEL RAILWAYS (USA)

Bermuda

Azores

argasso Sea

et the AMERICAN PRESIDENTS IN MINIATURE at the residents Hall of Fame (USA)

Caribbean Sea

There are enough building materials in the scenery to make about 40 full-size houses.

Some of the bridges contain 25,000 tiny pieces of wood!

Hundreds of mini people, each only a few centimeters tall, populate Northlandz.

Northlandz was built over 16 years by Bruce Williams Zaccagnino, who began the railroad as a hobby in his basement.

DISCOVER ONE OF THE WORLD'S LARGEST

MODEL RAILWAYS

With over 100 trains, 8 miles of track, 3,000 buildings, and half a million little trees, Northlandz Model Railroad in Flemington, New Jersey, is one of the largest model railways in the world. In this vast miniature world, tiny trains emerge from dark tunnels, speeding along rocky cliff-sides and across steep canyons, past pocket-sized people, teeny towns, and small-scale skyscrapers. All aboard for an adventure!

FALL UNDER A SPELL AT THE
FAIRY CASTLE

At Chicago's Museum of Science and Industry, you will discover the most lavish dollhouse in the world. Measuring 8 feet tall, with diamond-encrusted chandeliers, tiny gold cutlery, marble floors, and miniature works of art, the Fairy Castle is a palace fit for a pocket-sized princess. Created in the 1930s by silent film star Colleen Moore, the castle took seven years to complete and cost half a million dollars—which is equal to about seven million dollars today!

In the prince's bedroom, there's a "bearskin" rug made from ermine fur and mouse teeth!

The drawing room has a painting of Mickey and Minnie Mouse donated by Walt Disney.

Some tiny glass slippers are on display, measuring just 6 millimeters!

Over 100 architects, designers, and artists from around the world worked on the Fairy Castle.

CHICAGO, USA

In the bathroom, the bath is made of silver, and real water can flow from the dolphins' mouths!

The tapestries in the dining room have stitches so small they can only be seen under a microscope.

TAKE A PEEK AT ONE OF THE
WORLD'S SMALLEST BUTTERFLIES

On the salt marshes of the southwestern United States, keen-eyed nature lovers may spy one of the tiniest butterflies on the planet. The western pygmy blue has a wingspan of only 1.2 centimeters—it's the size of a fingernail! This little gem flutters close to the ground, so it's easy to miss unless you look very carefully.

Blink and you'll miss it!

The pygmy blue butterfly slurps up nectar from flowers using a long feeding tube.

Pygmy blue caterpillars have a useful relationship with ants. They produce a sweet liquid for the ants to eat, and in return, the ants protect them from predators.

SEND A LETTER WITH THE
WORLD'S SMALLEST POSTAL SERVICE

When artist Lea Redmond was waking up from a nap one day, the idea of a teeny, tiny letter popped into her head. She is now postmaster of the World's Smallest Post Service: a San Francisco–based business that makes itty-bitty letters for people to send to their loved ones all around the world. As well as letters, they make tiny greetings cards, invitations, and gifts, and have even sent a few miniature marriage proposals!

If you think someone is cute as a button, send a button in a mini parcel.

Send someone a tiny compass to tell them you'd be lost without them!

Each letter is fastened with a fairy-sized wax seal.

34

Before the letters are posted, they are sealed inside a larger envelope so they don't get lost in the mail.

SAN FRANCISCO, USA

Mexico

Cuba

Bahamas

Haiti

Dominican Republic

St. Kitts & Nevis

Antigua & Barbuda

Dominica

Saint Lucia

Barbados

Grenada

Trinidad & To

Jamaica

Belize

Guatemala

Honduras

El Salvador

Nicaragua

Costa Rica

Caribbean Sea

Panama

Venezuela

Guyana

Suriname

Size up the SMALLEST BIRD IN THE WORLD (Cuba)

Colombia

Look out for the tiny PATU DIGUA SPIDER (Colombia)

Galápagos Islands

Ecuador

Braz

Dive for tadpoles with the AMERICAN PYGMY KINGFISHER (Peru)

Peru

South Pacific Ocean

Find TINY TREASURES at the Alasitas Festival of Minatures (Bolivia)

Bolivia

Paraguay

Chile

Argentina

Uruguay

Stroke a MINIATURE FALABELLA HORSE (Argentina)

Falkland Islands

CENTRAL & SOUTH AMERICA

This continent is famous for amazing wildlife, so it's no surprise that here you'll find some of the tiniest creatures on the planet.

e away with one of the LITTLEST LIZARDS IN THE WORLD (Dominican Republic)

Meet the world's smallest monkey, the PYGMY MARMOSET (Brazil)

South
Atlantic
Ocean

LITTLEST LIZARDS IN THE WORLD

Deep in the forests of the remote island of Beata, in the Dominican Republic, lives a rare and special creature. Measuring only 1.6 centimeters long from nose to tail tip, the dwarf gecko is one of the smallest reptiles on Earth. This tiny lizard spends its days hiding away among damp leaves on the forest floor. It weighs only 0.2 grams, which is about the same as seven grains of rice!

The dwarf gecko is small enough to curl up on a coin.

This lizard is so small that if it left its damp habitat, it would quickly dry out and shrivel up.

If a predator grabs a gecko by the tail, the gecko can leave its tail behind and make a getaway, growing a new one later!

DOMINICAN REPUBLIC

Beata

The bee hummingbird must feed constantly to gain enough energy to survive. It eats over half its body weight in food per day!

This tiny dynamo can fly for 20 hours without stopping.

Despite its size, this hummingbird can fly at speeds of 30 miles per hour.

SMALLEST BIRD IN THE WORLD

Hovering among the flowers of Cuba's colorful forests is the bee hummingbird. It measures only 2.3 inches long and weighs just 1.6 grams, which is about half the weight of a dime! The smallest bird in the world also has the smallest nest in the world (the size of a thimble) and lays the smallest egg in the world (the size of a pea)!

This amazing bird can flap its wings 80 times per second, which is faster than the human eye can see.

CUBA

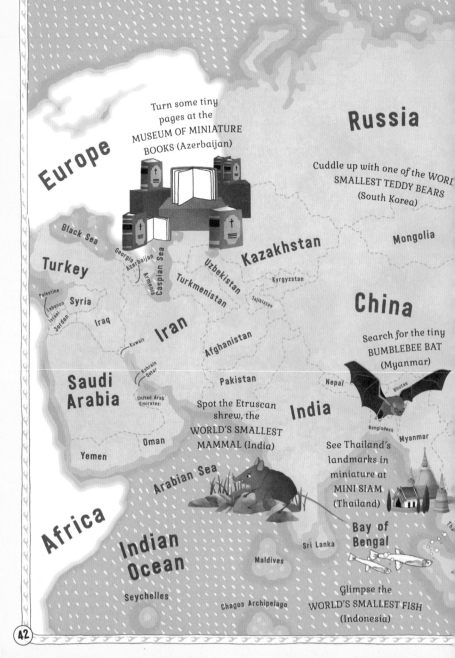

Turn some tiny pages at the MUSEUM OF MINIATURE BOOKS (Azerbaijan)

Russia

Cuddle up with one of the WORLD'S SMALLEST TEDDY BEARS (South Korea)

Europe

Black Sea

Georgia Azerbaijan Armenia Caspian Sea

Turkey

Kazakhstan

Uzbekistan

Mongolia

Palestine
Lebanon
Israel
Syria
Jordan
Iraq

Turkmenistan

Kyrgyzstan

Kuwait

Iran

Tajikistan

China

Afghanistan

Search for the tiny BUMBLEBEE BAT (Myanmar)

Bahrain
Qatar

Saudi Arabia

Pakistan

Nepal

Bhutan

United Arab Emirates

India

Spot the Etruscan shrew, the WORLD'S SMALLEST MAMMAL (India)

Oman

Bangladesh

Myanmar

Yemen

See Thailand's landmarks in miniature at MINI SIAM (Thailand)

Arabian Sea

Africa

Bay of Bengal

Indian Ocean

Sri Lanka

Maldives

Seychelles

Chagos Archipelago

Glimpse the WORLD'S SMALLEST FISH (Indonesia)

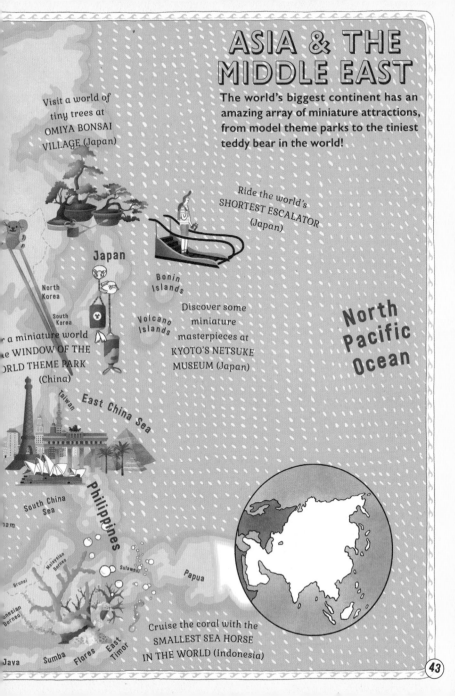

ASIA & THE MIDDLE EAST

The world's biggest continent has an amazing array of miniature attractions, from model theme parks to the tiniest teddy bear in the world!

Visit a world of tiny trees at OMIYA BONSAI VILLAGE (Japan)

Ride the world's SHORTEST ESCALATOR (Japan)

Japan

North Korea

South Korea

Bonin Islands

Volcano Islands

Discover some miniature masterpieces at KYOTO'S NETSUKE MUSEUM (Japan)

North Pacific Ocean

r a miniature world
e WINDOW OF THE
ORLD THEME PARK
(China)

Taiwan

East China Sea

South China Sea

am

Philippines

Brunei

Malaysian Borneo

Sulawesi

Papua

onesian Borneo

Java

Sumba

Flores

East Timor

Cruise the coral with the SMALLEST SEA HORSE IN THE WORLD (Indonesia)

43

The bonsai village contains thousands of miniature trees. There are several different bonsai nurseries and a museum.

Styles of Bonsai Tree

Formal upright
Informal upright
Slanting

Windswept
Cascade
Forest

44

VISIT A WORLD OF TINY TREES AT

OMIYA
BONSAI VILLAGE

On the outskirts of Tokyo lies a peaceful neighborhood that seems a million miles away from the bustle of the city. This is Omiya Bonsai Village, where patient gardeners spend many hours nurturing thousands of miniature trees. Bonsai trees are kept small by careful pruning and wiring throughout their lives. Some bonsais can live to be over 1,000 years old!

The Japanese word bonsai means "planted in a container."

Omiya Bonsai Village was set up in 1925 when a group of bonsai gardeners moved here from Tokyo after an earthquake.

TOKYO, JAPAN

KYOTO, JAPAN

The Netsuke Museum is housed in a building constructed for samurai (Japanese warriors) in 1820.

Netsuke depict people, animals, mythical creatures, and more.

DISCOVER SOME MINIATURE MASTERPIECES AT
KYOTO'S NETSUKE MUSEUM

Hundreds of years ago in Japan, men wore small ornaments called *netsuke* as fasteners on their clothing. These objects were made out of ivory, wood, or porcelain, and were often very intricately carved. Today, the Netsuke Museum in Kyoto showcases hundreds of these miniature works of art, with plenty of magnifying glasses on hand so visitors can appreciate their finer details!

Traditional Japanese clothes had no pockets, so men carried things in pouches. A netsuke was used to fasten a pouch to a belt. It quickly became a hot fashion accessory!

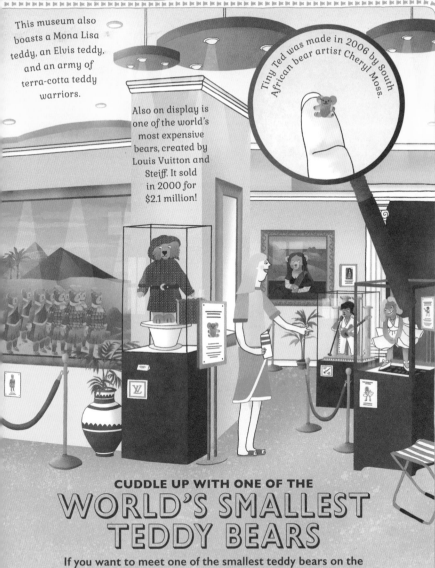

This museum also boasts a Mona Lisa teddy, an Elvis teddy, and an army of terra-cotta teddy warriors.

Tiny Ted was made in 2006 by South African bear artist Cheryl Moss.

Also on display is one of the world's most expensive bears, created by Louis Vuitton and Steiff. It sold in 2000 for $2.1 million!

CUDDLE UP WITH ONE OF THE
WORLD'S SMALLEST TEDDY BEARS

If you want to meet one of the smallest teddy bears on the planet, head to the Teddy Bear Museum on Jeju Island, South Korea. The size of a pea, Tiny Ted is only 4.5 millimeters high. This miniature marvel was stitched in exactly the same way as a larger teddy, so he has jointed arms and legs and a head that can swivel. Don't breathe too deeply when you're close to him, as you might inhale him!

49

CRUISE THE CORAL WITH THE
SMALLEST SEA HORSE IN THE WORLD

Satomi's pygmy sea horse is possibly the tiniest sea horse on Earth, measuring a mere 14 millimeters in length, which is smaller than a penny. This minuscule fish lives among the coral reefs off Indonesia's Derawan Islands. It wasn't discovered until 2008, partly because it is so tiny, and partly because it is nocturnal, hiding away during the day. Eagle-eyed divers, take note!

Satomi's sea horse is the smallest sea horse found so far, but there might be tinier species out there...

Adult Satomi's pygmy sea horses are small, but their offspring are even smaller. When they hatch, they are the size of an apostrophe!

The sea horse is one of the only creatures where the male—not the female—carries the eggs and hatches the young.

DERAWAN ISLANDS, INDONESIA

AUSTRALASIA & OCEANIA

From tiny desert fish to hidden garden gnomes and little hobbit houses, Australasia has its fair share of quirky mini marvels.

Seek out the WORLD'S SMALLEST FROG (Papua New Guinea)

Papua New Guinea

Indonesia

Visit STRELLEY POOL, home of microscopic fossils from 3.4 billion years ago (Australia)

Christmas Island

Steer clear of the tiny but deadly IRUKANDJI JELLYFISH (Austral

Australia

Survive in the outback with the DESERT GOBY (Australia)

Explore the mini village COCKINGTON GREEN GARDENS (Australia)

Take the plunge with the LITTLE PENGUIN (Australia)

Flinders Island

Tasmania

Search for hiding garden gnomes at the ASHCOMBE MAZE (Australia)

Hawaiian Islands

Federated States
of Micronesia

Marshall
Islands

South
Pacific
Ocean

Tuvalu

Solomon
Islands

New
Caledonia   Vanuatu

French
Polynesia

Marvel at the little lights
of the WAITOMO
GLOWWORM CAVES
(New Zealand)

Fiji   Samoa

Tonga

Visit Middle Earth
with a HOBBITON
MOVIE SET TOUR
(New Zealand)

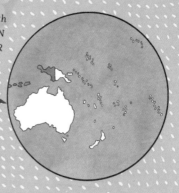

New
Zealand

Hike the hills
and stop off at a
MINIATURE HUT
(New Zealand)

PAPUA NEW GUINEA

13

This little frog hides among dead leaves on the forest floor. The male's mating call sounds like that of an insect, making it very difficult to track down.

SEEK OUT THE
WORLD'S SMALLEST FROG

In August 2009, scientists working in an area of rain forest in Papua New Guinea made a very big discovery. Or you could say it was a very small discovery: the littlest frog ever found. Measuring less than 7.7 millimeters—the same size as a fly—*Paedophryne amauensis* is not only the world's smallest frog, it is also the smallest animal with a backbone ever discovered. A large claim to fame for a very tiny creature!

This tiny creature can jump a whopping 30 times its body length!

Unlike some other frogs, this creature has no tadpole stage—it hatches as a "hopper": a mini version of the adult.

This little battler can leave the water for a short time, flipping across moist patches of land to get to a new puddle.

AUSTRALIA

The desert goby can survive in water three times saltier than seawater!

SURVIVE IN THE OUTBACK WITH THE
DESERT GOBY

Although only two inches long, the desert goby is a tough survivor. This little fish lives in pools in the Australian outback and can withstand temperatures from as low as 40 degrees to a blistering 104 degrees Fahrenheit! When the scarce rains fall, the goby uses small trickles of water to slither from one muddy puddle to another. In this way, it can travel hundreds of miles across the desert in search of a mate. Not bad for a tiny fish!

This fish is only a few inches long, but it can travel vast distances.

If there is a flood, the goby can anchor itself to the rocks using its fins so it doesn't get washed away.

South Orkney Islands

Dive with the FUR SEAL, smallest of all the Antarctic seals (South Shetland Islands)

South Shetland Islands

Escape the crowds with the SMALLEST POPULATION ON EARTH

Southern Ocean

Weddell Sea

Meet the tiny ANTARCTIC MIDGE: the only insect on the continent (Marguerite Bay)

Ronne Ice Shelf

Antarctica

Bellingshausen Sea

Marvel at the DRIEST PLACE ON EARTH (Dry Valleys)

Amundsen Sea

Ross Ice Shelf

Grab a light lunch with the ANTARCTIC KRILL (Amundsen Sea)

Patrol the ocean floor with the ANTARCTIC SEA PIG (Ross Sea)

Ross Sea

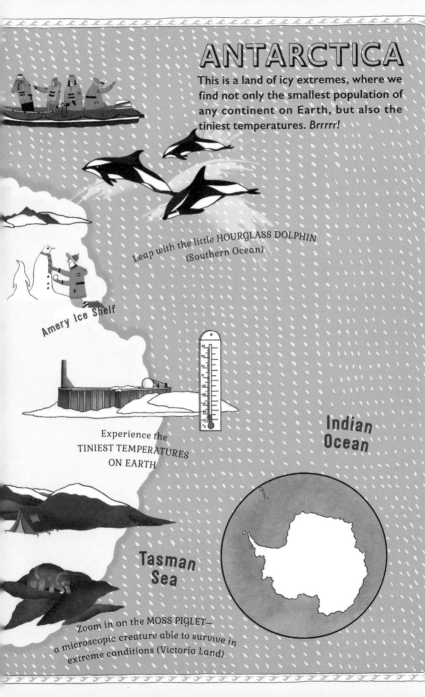

ANTARCTICA

This is a land of icy extremes, where we find not only the smallest population of any continent on Earth, but also the tiniest temperatures. *Brrrrr!*

Leap with the little HOURGLASS DOLPHIN
(Southern Ocean)

Amery Ice Shelf

Experience the
TINIEST TEMPERATURES
ON EARTH

Indian
Ocean

Tasman
Sea

Zoom in on the MOSS PIGLET—
a microscopic creature able to survive in
extreme conditions (Victoria Land)

59

The digestive system of a krill is often bright green because of all the tiny plants it eats.

Krill can live for up to seven years, which is surprising considering the number of animals that feed on them.

The total weight of all the Antarctic krill on Earth is thought to be more than the total weight of all humans!

At certain times of the year, Antarctic krill gather in swarms so large they can be seen from space.

GRAB A LIGHT LUNCH WITH THE
ANTARCTIC KRILL

Small in size but huge in importance, Antarctic krill are the engine that powers the Antarctic food chain. These tiny, shrimp-like creatures measure only about two inches long, but they gather in enormous swarms, numbering millions. Most of the animals in the Antarctic—whales, seals, birds, and fish—depend on krill as a key part of their diet. Each day, a single blue whale can guzzle over 4 tons of krill—that's the same weight as an African elephant!

SOUTHERN OCEAN

CAN YOU FIND?

There are so many miniature things to spot throughout this book—not just the bonsai trees or the fairy castle that first sent you on your adventures. See if you can remember where you've spotted the items below, and go back to these destinations to find them. What other things can you spot along the way?

Firefighters, **Bekonscot**

Windmill, **Madurodam**

Neon snail, **Berlin**

Stegosaurus, **Lyon**

Penguins, **Vienna**

Snake, **Madagascar**

Butterfly, **Namibia**

Signalman, **Northlandz**

Ferris wheel, **Northlandz**

Harp, **Fairy Castle**

Caterpillar, **Southwest USA**

Sealing wax, **San Francisco**

Parakeet, **Dominican Republic**

Hummingbird nest, **Cuba**

Cascade bonsai, **Omiya**

Whale netsuke, **Kyoto**

Space teddy, **South Korea**

Six sea horses, **Indonesia**

Tiger parrot, **Papua New Guinea**

Budgerigar, **Australia**

Bourke's parrot, **Australia**

OTHER TITLES IN THE ATLAS OF ADVENTURES SERIES

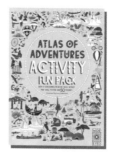

First published in the U.S.A. in 2017 by
Wide Eyed Editions, an imprint of Quarto Inc.,
276 Fifth Avenue, Suite 206, New York, NY 10001
QuartoKnows.com
Visit our blogs at QuartoKnows.com

Atlas of Animal Adventures copyright © Aurum Press Ltd 2016
Illustrations copyright © Lucy Letherland 2016

All rights reserved.
No part of this publication may be reproduced, stored in a retrieval system, or transmitted, in any
form, or by any means, electrical, mechanical, photocopying, recording or otherwise without the
prior written permission of the publisher or a license permitting restricted copying.

A catalog record for this book is available from the British Library.

ISBN 978-1-84780-910-0

Illustrated with colored inks
Set in Festivo, Gabriela, and Gill Sans Shadow

Designed by Joe Hales and Andrew Watson
Published by Rachel Williams

Printed in China

1 3 5 7 9 8 6 4 2

MIX
Paper from
responsible sources
FSC® C104723